Voice
FROM THE
HEART

Walk with the Spirit

DAVID KLINE

Copyright © 2021 by David Kline

All rights reserved. No part of this book may be used or reproduced by any means, graphic, electronic or mechanical, including photocopying, recording, taping or by any information storage retrieval system, without the written permission of the author, except in the case of brief quotations embodied in reviews.

Paperback ISBN 978-1-945169-69-4

Published by
Orison Publishers, Inc.
PO Box 188, Grantham, PA 17027
www.OrisonPublishers.com

Scripture quotations are taken from the King James Version of the Bible. Public domain.

All interior images are provided by Skylar Kline.

For in my cries are my *tears filled with love*
As He is in me and I am in Him
Feeling His *mercy and compassion*
That I am saved.

Contents

Acknowledgments vii
Introduction ix
Special Note xv

Part I: Accepting Wisdom 3
Come to Me 5
Trinity of Spirit: Heart, Mind and Soul 6
Peace from Within 7
When Anger Speaks 8
Silence in Praise 9
Reflection of the Soul 10
Eternal Light 11
Give Thy Gift and Receive 12
Creator-Blessed 13
Joyous Spirit and Thankful Heart 14

Part II: Asking for Grace 17
Daily Bread 18
Direct My Steps 19
Fear Not, For I Am with You 20
Perfect Light unto My Path 21
Speak to Thy Heart 22
Bless Me, Jesus, to Be a Child at Heart 23
Hand of Compassion 24
Trinity's Touch 25
The Garden 26
Promise of the Spirit 27

Part III: Keeping Faith 31
Thy Brother 33
The Journey 34
The Cross and the Stone 35
Thy Prayers, Even If Delayed, Are Answered, Never Denied ... 36
Eyes of Faith 37
Angels' Slumber 38

When Evil Knocks 39
Lift Thy Burdens 40
Light of the Lord 41
Cobwebs 42

Part IV: Receiving Love 45
Step to Heaven 46
Love of Joy 47
Gift of Passion and Purpose 48
Love Thyself 49
Refresh My Soul 50
Devil's Shadow 51
Thy Spirit of Peace and Love 52
Heart of Fire 53
Thy Need Fulfilled 54
Voice from the Heart 55

Part V: Embracing the Spirit 59
Redemption 60
Essence Divine 61
Green Pasture 62
Together We Pray 63
Rise Up in Spirit 64

Special Inspirations 67
That Man Is You! (TMIY) 68
The Woman in Faith (TWIF) 69

Conclusion 73
References 75
Notes 80

Acknowledgments

To my mother, who always gave me the confidence to believe in myself when others would not. She inspired me to go on, and she held a belief in me that I would do something special and make her proud. I dedicate this book to her in "Loving Memory" for giving me a faith to carry and an inspiration to follow.

To my wife Karen, who sensed that my writings were something special. She felt my emotional connection within the prayers and the love of joy they represented. I had to hold her back from wanting to edit them as I was writing them. I had to joke with her that it was interfering with my flow and train of thought during my creative process. Out of love and respect, her support is more appreciated than I can ever express.

To my daughter Skylar, who sees beauty and was able to capture with her lens the passion I wanted to express in my words from the *heart* and share with others.

Special thanks go to Paradisus Dei for the program "That Man Is You," which opened up my eyes and gave me insights into my faith with passion, conviction and clarity, helping me to discover that, as men, we are duty bound to live our life for the good of society and to show love, kindness and compassion in all that we do.

Blessings to the men of "All Saints Parish," who stepped forward to hear the message of what it is to be a man of faith in these times of turmoil and uncertainty. I owe a special thanks to them for helping me not to be afraid to share my gift of prayer and for encouraging me and supporting me in putting all these inspirations /prayers together in a book so that others may receive comfort from reading and hearing them as they have.

I thank all the sources that gave me support and encouragement in writing these *prayers of reflection, contemplation and inspiration* for this book.

Introduction

Prayer can have deep *spiritual* undertones in one's life. We see this in both the Old and New Testaments of the Bible. One aspect of prayer is the freedom it gives us to explore and open our minds. Prayer gives us both a *spiritual connection* and a physical connection at the same time when we feel and sense the presence of God. Prayer also helps to relax the mind and, for some, aids them in entering a mild meditative state.

The beauty of prayer is that it is both simplistic and complex at the same time. For example, one can say a few words, such as "Thank You, Jesus," or go into more depth and use many words. Prayer can be shaped and molded to fit into one's emotions and to express the deepest, innermost feelings. Prayer can be dry and unemotional or full of joy and tenderness. Prayer can be like the greatest love poem or the saddest sonnet. Prayer can be said in silence or expressed outwardly with others. Prayer is not something to be ashamed of; rather, it is a joyous gift given to us to interact in spirit with Jesus.

Prayer is a *spiritual essence* within us that gives us *peace and harmony* to grow and embrace the *richness and fullness of life*. For Jesus, prayer was an act of communicating with the Father and loving life. In the *spirit of love*, prayer is tied to the heart and is a key to unlock the *soul and open the mind to the mysteries of the universe* that we seek. I contend that prayer can give one a strong *spiritual focus* and understanding.

The *power of prayer* can give one a focus into insights that may seem strange but that delve into the mysteries of faith. In the Gospels, Jesus speaks in parables to those around Him so they could understand, but He tells His disciples what He really meant. So, too, it is with the *mysteries of faith*; they are like the parables of the Gospels whose meanings need to be opened to us. In prayer, with reflection, the true meaning can come to us.

With the *Spirit as our guide to walk us through*, prayer joins the *spirit* as the student listening to the teacher. Compare to the disciples listening to Jesus and Jesus listening to the Father. Prayer helps tune our thoughts to those of Jesus for a higher power as we become more open to understand. Prayer is a visible mystery that both lies before us and has been with us. Prayer is powerful and unique and a wonderful *mystery of faith* given to us. One just needs to use it to unlock the power within.

Have you ever wondered about the so-called "inner voice" that we hear? With prayer and reflection we can hear that soft voice within us, calming and comforting us. This voice acts as a guiding counselor for us. Prayer helps us to focus and calm the mind. Given all the modern distractions around us, slowing down to relax and pray doesn't seem so appealing. However, one of the greatest benefits of prayer is the stress-reducing effects it has to offer.

Setting aside a quiet time for yourself with prayer allows you this calming touch. Giving yourself just five minutes to start with can produce results. Lack of time is often used as an excuse for not praying. But even taking five minutes for prayer when you first get up or before you go to bed can work. You must make an effort to find time for prayer. *The key is to make your alone time free from interruptions and distractions.* The more time you take for prayer, the stronger the voice can become. The idea is that it is not so much the time you spend in prayer that is effective as the quality of it. Spending quality time to build a relationship with Jesus in prayer is the starting point to allowing that inner voice (the voice of the heart) to prosper.

Each of us has a view about prayer. Some see prayer as something to do, while others view prayer as a fundamental part of life. Prayer is said to be able to do many things, such as healing, giving guidance and being calming, for example. Prayer does all these things and more. A *power of prayer* does exist in each of us, but it is something that needs to be nurtured. The *power of prayer* is subtle or hidden within us at first, but it can grow like the tiny mustard seed into a large, overshadowing force.

Too often we miss the value of prayer within our daily lives; we overlook the hidden treasures of what it has to offer us.

Through the call of *faith* one turns to prayer as a devotion, but at other times one turns to prayer to fulfill an emotional need and for support. My experience with prayer was one of finding a way to cope with the stress of life and the loss of close family members. On my journey to understanding and using prayer, I found that it helped me unlock a written expression held deep within myself. Even though my writings come from a Catholic perspective, they embrace the innermost feelings within the Christian heart!

I came to realize and started to accept that this hidden talent I had was being brought out for a higher purpose. I understand the impact my writings have upon others because they *come from the heart* and are a true expression of both the deep turmoil and the love that we all have within us. I wish to point out that I am a simple layman with a *clarity of thought* that allows me to write with special passion, feeling, insight and purpose within this book. My gift is to share with others and let them discover the joy I have found in writing these inspirations given to me by the Holy Spirit.

Coming to understand and accept prayer has led me on an extraordinary journey. This book is a collection of inspirations, reflections and prayers that were written to fulfill a need, to say and express what is held within our hearts as we are touched by the Father.

You will find that these readings can be deeply personal, emotional and uplifting. You can use them daily at any time to gather strength and courage from the Lord. The Spirit will reach out to you as you begin your journey in the practice of a daily prayer life and build it into a habit. This book is meant to give you, the reader, inspiration and faith in starting, building or maintaining your spiritual growth with prayer. My goal is to help people open up to prayer and encourage them to understand it, use it and benefit from it. May this book bring comfort, joy and love into your heart from the Spirit and love of Jesus.

Let us take a journey together as we explore the mysteries of faith in prayer.

Let your heart
be a voice to guide you.

Special Note

To set the stage, before you read the inspiration/prayer, I want you, the reader, to first read the section titled "Narration." This section gives some insight into what the inspiration/prayer is about.

I have found it helpful to relax and clear the mind first, freeing the mind to pull together images/pictures and to visualize a happy, peaceful setting. After you are relaxed and have visualized a calming setting in your mind, read the narration.

Read each narration slowly, letting the words sink in and feeling their meaning as you place yourself within the narration. Like a good story, let the reading embrace you and capture the moment.

Once you are in the moment, read the inspiration/prayer, letting your thoughts and feelings grasp the words to acquire any hidden insights. Have an open heart and mind to understand and sense the joy and passion of Jesus.

Reflection is wisdom of the soul.

Part I
Accepting Wisdom

**Pray with *passion* to the Father,
for His wisdom will fill your soul!**

What is wisdom to us? Most of us think of wisdom as an awareness of something and having more knowledge of it than another. According to Webster's dictionary, wisdom is the "ability to discern inner qualities and relationships: insight; good sense: judgment; a wise attitude, belief, or course of action."(1)

The King James Version of the Bible says:

> *If any of you lack wisdom, let him ask of God, that giveth to all men liberally, and upbraideth not [without fault]; and it shall be given him (James 1:5).*

> *That the God of our Lord Jesus Christ, the Father of glory, may give unto you the spirit of wisdom and revelation in the knowledge of him (Ephesians 1:17).*

Wisdom also can be a spiritual knowledge that one receives when contemplating a reading, verse or passage. With prayer, wisdom develops into understanding something at a higher level. This can be a thought that occurs to us or a picture of something that we see in which a deep understanding occurs to us of what it may mean. Although most of us think wisdom is learned by or through experience, it can be taught to us also. King Solomon requested that God give him a "great mind of wisdom." From Proverbs, King Solomon teaches us wisdom in the ways of the Lord. The Scriptures are full of knowledge and wisdom for us to follow. Wisdom starts with being willing to have an *open heart* to listen to the words of the Lord. Each of the readings in this section have a special wisdom if you listen to and let the words flow into your heart.

Come to Me

NARRATION

The voice of the Lord is always near for us to hear. When one is calm and undisturbed, the voice of the Lord shall come and be heard. In the *Spirit of the Lord*, can one find direction to bring peace and love into the heart?

Inspiration

In my dream, I hear Jesus's whisper to my ear, "Come to Me, come to Me, come to Me." He says to me, "I know you are the 'imperfect Man,' full of sin, guilt and pride, but I want you to be at My side! From where you come there is no shame to bear; heed My call unto My Father's care. In you shall I make as a stone like no other, as full of marble and crystalline white, that you shall take My words for all to know their future is bright. Go now to speak and write of peace and love to this world, for you are My messenger I send through Heaven above!"

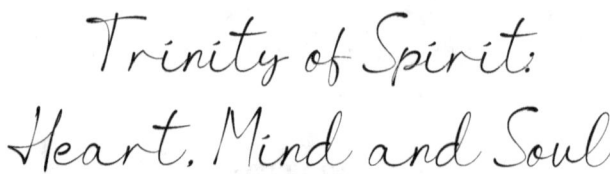

Trinity of Spirit: Heart, Mind and Soul

NARRATION

The S*pirit is a blessing* that comes to each of us when we are open to understand. It *offers a light unto the soul* to receive wisdom and compassion, pushing us toward a life of *love and purpose* to find our *Divinity*.

Prayer of Contemplation

From the heart, to the mind, through the soul, does the spirit go! To rise in spirit, we must embrace and accept it. The spirit's touch is ever so slight; it enters a gentle heart, calming the mind, quieting thoughts so we feel internal wisdom calling out. Moving to rise in passion deep within the soul do we feel the spirit's strength and heavenly might. Amen, I say, to this "trinity of spirit" that passes to us all, to give one its blessing and glory of eternal light!

Amen!

Peace from Within

NARRATION

Jesus taught with many parables and from the proverbs of King Solomon. He notes that one can master strife to live a joyous life.(2) We all have internal struggles that we face throughout the day. In asking for patience and taking a moment to become calm, we overcome a stressful situation and, like the wise man, set folly aside.

Inspiration

To summon strength from within is an enduring task…for the prudent man knows that humility will overcome intemperance. To be tested in time of trial *will require great patience, courage and strong focus of mind to keep one true.* To see that which is the beginning and to know its end—here springs eternal knowledge granted to him the wise man, who stands guard to turn away his folly and is given peace to himself within!

When Anger Speaks

NARRATION

Anger is not a true emotion within us. Anger is something that we let build in us that brings out hostility, as many of the proverbs of King Solomon point out.(3) We can empty out this emotion so it has no effect on us, for a calm mind is not fooled or easily misled by what *anger* can do. We have control over this unnatural emotion if we choose to see it for what it is and push it aside.

Prayer of Contemplation

With the tongue we lash out, before we know what is said. Experiencing the hurt that unkind words can cause is a *pain* not so easily forgiven. With *anger, emotion takes over the rational thought* to push forward in haste. To squelch *anger* one must ask, "Are my actions worthy to this task?" A *man slow to anger* and able to hold back unjust words is mightier than an army in battle. King Solomon made known, in his wisdom, that "anger is our foe," an emotion that each man can overcome from within. So I ask, "Praise be to God above, remove this *anger that speaks* and put forth *humility in my heart* so that calm and peace will forever reign upon this house."

Amen!

Silence in Praise

NARRATION

One must try to set aside time to be alone in the presence of the Lord. During this time of internal thought and silence, can we reflect on the glory of Jesus? When we do, His guidance that we seek will come to us, so that we will be filled with His love and understanding.

Prayer of Reflection

As Jesus went to pray alone in silence, may I, too, go to a place of quiet meditation away from all the noise of the *devil's distractions*. "Lord, let me be still to hear Your voice and conptemplate the power of Your presence and wonders of Your works. May You fill me as the empty vessel that I am before You, Lord, with Your wisdom, peace and grace! Give me courage and direction that *I may but listen in silence for the answers to my troubles and sorrows, answers that come from Your divine spiritual love for me!* I ask this in the name of Your Son, Jesus Christ."

Amen!

Reflection of the Soul

NARRATION

We each come to crossroads in our life. Behind us is the *past* and ahead of us is the *future*, but before us now *is the present*; this is when we decide what to do. In everything we do is the *choice of the now*. To be in *reflection of thought* is most comforting, for this is when the *Holy Spirit will guide us toward the direction we must go*. To *cross our bridge and to follow our river of destiny* does the Lord lead us, onward to His most *heavenly favor* to receive His peace and love upon the soul.

Prayer of Reflection

Where the *past leads to the future* is where we meet the *present*. For this is the *bridge of life's journey,* the reflection of the soul! Down below in the quiet flow is the river that is *destiny*. The ripples and the waves of the water are our *life's ups and downs*. Sit in reflection of things past and of those yet to come, for in the now is the *gift that is the present*. Truly, I say, a watchful man guards his steps, but a foolish one will stumble. Give *thanks and praise* to the Lord, for *He is the Master of each one's destiny!* Amen! Amen, I say, that Jesus be our guide to help us cross our *bridge and follow that destiny toward the Lord's glory*. In this I pray, that all may see my Lord Jesus, to guide them each day.

Amen!

Eternal Light

NARRATION

When our thoughts and minds are focused, we can understand as we let ourselves be open to receive. Miracles happen that sometimes cannot be explained as we accept the unknown and have no fear. Such is the case of the *Holy Spirit*, that force which guides us all, leading us to do things we never thought possible or protecting us in unseen ways. The *Spirit is in all of us to give inspiration, guidance and, most of all, love* as we embrace it within our *heart*!

Prayer of Inspiration

"O Holy Spirit, protector in day and guardian through the night, let me come into Your *most holy light,* that I may see, feel, know and love what is right! A holy bounty of endless might Thy Spirit gives that all shall live and understand. From 'age to age,' the Spirit has no end that it shall extend throughout this world in every place and time to make every moment *Thine.*" Let my spirit grasp the soul to follow, giving a heart full of peace and love that glows for all to see! For this heart of love shall the Spirit bring a flame as from the center of the sun that burns to lead us out of darkness toward a glory eternal and forever bright!

Amen!

Give Thy Gift and Receive

NARRATION

In the Gospels, Jesus gives His gift of the Holy Spirit to the apostles.(4) The Holy Spirit bestows its unique gifts to each apostle to share with others. Therefore, one should expect each person in *union with the Holy Spirit* to have his or her own unique gift that is meant to be shared. As Jesus directed the apostles to use their gifts, so, too, does the Holy Spirit do so within us, as this is the wisdom of the Lord.

Prayer of Inspiration

To stand against the *tide* when others turn away requires courage of the *soul*. To hold fast to a conviction when others want no part of it is the test that is placed upon us. Being true to *thyself* is that defining moment that the Lord has given. "Stay the course" is what the *heart* demands when all hope is abandoned. Joy shall come to him who *obeys his heart in love of the Lord* to follow the path that is given him. When others are blinded and do not see a just cause, the one who stands united in purpose will know the *great light of the Lord*. To thee I give these words of wisdom: *hold close to the heart your gifts that have been given*; accept them and share them with others even when they do not understand. You shall be the *spark of eternal light* that shall flicker within to grow in love until others' gifts shall be revealed and awakened. Truly, I say to you, each of you has a gift given to you that shall be opened and brought forth to share, receiving thy great blessings of the Lord!

Amen!

Creator-Blessed

NARRATION

Place in your mind how Job had everything taken away from him by the devil. In the story of Job, when he came back to regard God in his life, his blessings returned.(5) We are like that in life sometimes when we turn away from God; but when we return to Jesus and the Father, great blessings fall upon us. With wisdom and thankfulness in our hearts, this prayer recognizes that we are all given many things in life. As in the Old Testament, the Jewish people were told to remember the Lord always and to give thanks. This prayer is a reminder of the covenant that we have as Christians with Jesus, to be thankful for what we have and that we are His humble servants.

Prayer of Inspiration

"Thank You for this day, Jesus, and for the many blessings You have bestowed upon me. May You fill me with Your strength, courage and wisdom to confront the challenges I will face throughout this Your blessed day. Lord, let me give honor and praise unto You all my days. O Heavenly Father, let me always remember and never forget all that I have is a great gift that comes from You. May Your blessings continue to flow unto me, this Your loving, humble servant, as I give thanks to Thy name, God the Almighty Father."

Amen!

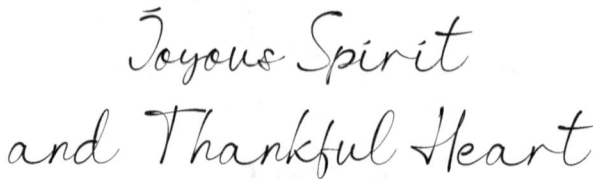

Joyous Spirit and Thankful Heart

NARRATION

From the Book of Daniel in the Old Testament, Daniel always praises and thanks the Lord. From his prayerful soul he gathers his strength and gains in wisdom to have the *eyes of faith*. Daniel is always thankful in his heart for whatever the Lord asks. He maintains a *joyous spirit to garner the blessings of the Lord*. From this we can learn that a joyous spirit and a thankful heart can lead us to overcome our struggles.(6)

Prayer of Contemplation

"A *joyous spirit* must one have to receive the fullness of life and to recognize Thy gifts laid before them, to cause the *eyes of faith* be opened, springing out from the prayerful soul!" Truly, I say to you, a hardened *heart* will wither on the vine, but a *heart* that is willing and grateful shall receive the bounty of the Lord to which His great *blessings* flow! Amen! Amen, I say; "Let me not fall into despair, my Lord, but let me stay true to the *love of joy filled with my purpose* and let happiness enter as to always come forth from a thankful heart! To this end I ask, my Jesus, for that *joyous spirit* to forever be part of me in every task You give me to undertake."

Amen!

Amazing grace awaits all who ask.

Part II
Asking for Grace

Pray with *conviction* to honor thy Father, for His grace will come upon you!

Can we fathom what grace is? Webster's dictionary defines grace as "unmerited divine assistance given to humans for their regeneration or sanctification; a virtue coming from God."(7) We can think of grace also as a physical state of peace and calm received from a spiritual level in which we are touched to receive a heavenly/Divine honor.

In prayer, *grace* is an *essence of love* given to us by the Lord *Jesus Christ, God the Father and the Holy Spirit and shared through the Mother of Jesus, the Virgin Mary.* Grace is that feeling that touches the *heart* and brings us internal *joy* like no other. Many signs and miracles were performed by Jesus out of His compassion and eternal grace. The readings in this section let you feel the *love of grace* flow into the heart.

Daily Bread

NARRATION

Jesus often teaches us to have compassion and forgiveness for those around us. We free ourselves from the stress of despair and anguish when we can forgive. To enjoy life, one must be full of *happiness* (the joyous spirit) and share love with others that truly comes from the *heart*. These are what keep one fed and are our *daily bread*.

Prayer of Inspiration

In the *spirit* shall we become, for it is the Lord's will to be done. "I ask in Heaven, Jesus, send me forth to complete Your tasks. Lord, fill my *soul* with *compassion and forgiveness* and place a *joyous spirit* for life *full of love upon my heart*." Jesus taught that this would be a *daily bread* for each day, that all are forever fed on the journey toward life eternal!

Amen!

Direct My Steps

NARRATION

At times we feel uncertain in what to do. With an open heart and peace of mind, we can listen for answers to our questions. God's grace does come to those who take the time to listen and accept it, and it gives one courage to take action.

Prayer of Contemplation

"In aimless wonder do I tread, for where am I to go, my Lord? Set me straight onto the direction I must go, to fulfill my purpose and destiny given to me!" Truly, I say to you, the Lord's grace will **direct my steps** *for the journey*. It is by *faith* that mountains shall be but stepping stones along the way. "I give You *thanks and praise, O great Father who art in Heaven,* for You have shown me Your path to take." Amen! Amen, I say; my *Lord's path* is made known to all who have love in their heart and peace in their soul! In this I pray, to the *glory of my most blessed Lord Jesus Christ.*

Amen!

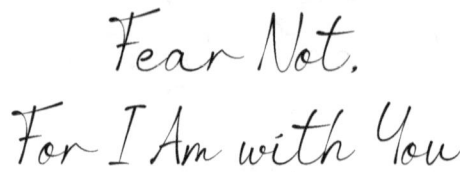

NARRATION

To be honest with ourselves requires courage because we see our weaknesses and know that evil is always pressing us. God gives us His grace to use and help us overcome our faults. We must be open to accepting God's grace and know that His love has no bounds and is never-ending.

Prayer of Reflection

When the shadow of *evil* is upon us, to whom do we turn? In this dark hour, the Lord calls to my soul to fear not! "Hearken to My word," I hear Him say; "I am with you always," as the Father speaks to His Son. "Heavenly Father, I am not worthy to stand in Your presence, and I beg forgiveness in what I have failed to do. In tears do I weep, for all that You have done for me that I give honor and paise in Your name." Truly, I say to you, "Let me be filled with the Holy Spirit, my Lord, and place me on the highest mountain to serve as a guiding light of Your glory." Amen! Amen, I say to the Father, "As You take away the evil upon my soul, that I should make a faithful servant, let courage and wisdom lead me always to do what is right and pleasing in Your sight. In this I ask, our most merciful Lord Jesus Christ."

Amen!

Perfect Light unto My Path

NARRATION

When we are in despair, we feel no hope to lift our spirit. With great faith giving us wisdom, all is possible; no troubles are too big to bear. We see this with Moses as he led his people in the desert, for he knew that the Lord would always be there; he had no doubt or fear. When we are most in need and believe in His works, all shall be given and received in the Spirit of the Lord.

Prayer of Contemplation

The lonely path of despair that I must walk is the cross that I am proud to bear—for my faith to be tested as in the days of Moses in the desert, to seek evermore until it be found! I ask *God's grace* to *come forth* to shine upon this humble servant who is *true in purpose and ever faithful to the Lord's desire.* Like the *empty vessel*, I shall be filled in *Spirit* to hold its *love in my heart*, that I receive the promise from my Lord for a new start. For full of *grace* I shall be, as Lazarus taken into the bosom of Abraham, forever blessed and free from my distress. To this I say *Amen*, that the Lord has sent me as an example that no trouble is too great. For He is with me, that *perfect Light, to set my path true and right.* Let me go forth in gratitude and praise, *accepting my Lord's embracing love for me all my days.*

Amen!

NARRATION

Being silent and listening for God's voice can be surprising. When we are calm and most open to Him, His words will come to us, guide us and give comfort to us. When we truly listen, we can understand and obtain the wisdom we seek to calm the soul and prepare for the task(s) laid before us.

Prayer of Inspiration

From the silence of *adoration*, I can feel the senses tingle with joy as I hear the words of the Lord come to me! Comfort do they bring when all is in doubt, to calm my *soul* and let fear fade away within. For I am told, "Do not despair," for the road ahead is not bare when the Lord *speaks to the heart*, sharing His presence along the way. With *thanks and praise*, amen, I say, to this day the Lord has given, that He is ever present to bestow His words of *wisdom and grace* upon me. For from His words I will feel, see and speak of His *love* evermore unto eternity.

Amen!

Bless Me, Jesus, to Be a Child at Heart

NARRATION

To stay simple in our mind like a child is to see the great blessings of Jesus. As Jesus taught, like a child we must be able to accept Him in our heart, for then His grace will come to us and His Spirit will guide us on His path.(8) To ask for blessing and favor is most pleasing to the Lord as we acknowledge Him and stay true to our heart.

Prayer of Inspiration

"Bless me, Jesus; fill my heart and soul with Your love and kindness. Let me see the glory of Your ways, that I may walk uprightly to follow You all my days. Amen, I say; blessed I be in spirit, as a child at heart, for it is to You, O Jesus, I come and forever belong. For love and peace I pray, and to bless me, my Jesus, with grace of mind, that I may be strong in faith and never stray away from You." In this I pray to the Lord our Savior Jesus Christ.

Amen!

Hand of Compassion

NARRATION

In the Gospels, Jesus teaches compassion through examples of His love and grace. One example is His compassion to make a blind man see.(9) From our asking and persistence in faith is Jesus calling us to reach out. He wants us to know that He is forever present and ready to lend a hand of compassion and relieve the burden from our heart.

Prayer of Reflection

When the weight of doubt comes crashing down upon me, do I feel crushed in unbelief? With eyes dazed and full of tears do I look up wondering what I have done. In the distance do I see a mist coming to consume me, as a voice echoes throughout my *soul*, calling me to "reach out to take My hand." From the mist I feel a grip ever so slight, but I know it is full of the Lord's might. For this is the *hand of compassion* from Jesus pulling me close to release my pain. Truly, I say to you, compassion will be given to all who reach out in faith without doubt. Amen! Amen, I say, as Jesus lives in *spirit,* He is always present throughout! Let us pray to receive always the greatest gift of *love and grace* from thy Jesus His everlasting compassion of *heart.*

Amen!

Trinity's Touch

NARRATION

The power of the Trinity is ever present for us to call upon; the Father, Son and Holy (Ghost) Spirit are never far to lift us up when we need it. The grace of the Trinity is with us when love and compassion freely flow from our heart toward others; then we feel an overwhelming sense of joy and internal happiness.

Prayer of Inspiration

"In the name of Jesus Christ, beloved Son, I beseech You to let the most *blessed, sacred, holy Trinity of the Father, Son and Holy Spirit* descend over me. May the holy Trinity touch my heart with endless love and compassion and pierce my soul with burning desire to know my Lord, as Your power, grace and glory be always evermore for eternity!"

Amen!

The Garden

NARRATION

When our minds are full of thoughts, we are distracted. Jesus taught that we must slow down the mind and listen for His joy. To be tranquil and at peace with ourselves is the first step into the Garden to hear the soft whisper of Jesus's call. Being alone and in solitude frees us from distractions. (10) Answers will come to all who can listen with an open heart and quiet mind to stand in joy of the Lord's presence.

Prayer of Contemplation

Do you not hear the rushing water over the rocks, the bees buzzing to the flowers, or the birds singing? The voice of the Master is near. In all things, big and small, are wonders given and shown. Give thanks and praise to listen with an open heart and ear. Truly, I say, shall the mind be silent that all shall become clear! Amen! Amen, I say; "Jesus, let me hear Your soft whisper ever so slight to be filled with grace of my Father's heavenly might! To this I pray, Lord, for Your garden of eternal joy be forever in my heart!"

Amen!

NARRATION

Through our faith many signs are given, but the greatest gift is the Holy Spirit. The Spirit guides us in all that we do and bestows its gift upon us that we may understand and follow our passion and purpose.

Prayer of Reflection

From Heaven above to the earth below, does the *Holy Spirit* oversee and guide us all. Great strength, wisdom and grace does the Spirit bestow when we are but open to its great call. From eyes closed will the blind man see, and from deaf ears and mute tongue will the deaf man speak as witness to the power and glory of the most *Holy Spirit*. So let us ask, "O come, Holy Spirit," and receive that it will be given to all who seek.

Amen!

Let your faith guide you
to open the door
of possibilities within you.

PART III
Keeping Faith

Pray with *humility* before the Father and Son and be strengthened in *faith*!

Faith can be said to be an unseen belief in something. Webster's dictionary defines faith as "belief and trust in and loyalty to God," "sincerity of intentions," "firm belief in something for which there is no proof," and "something that is believed especially with strong conviction."(11)

We often look to faith as a spiritual/unseen belief in a higher power, be it *God or a Supreme Creator as seen through the heart and mind of man.* Faith is to hold to a course of action and direction, never fearing what the outcome will be.

With *faith* we are called to believe in Jesus and the works of the Father. The Old Testament has stories of the *test of faith* being put to the Jews. In the New Testament, the Gospels also have stories or acts requesting *faith*, such as the woman touching Jesus's garment to be healed.(12)

Faith is that force that gives us the courage and strength to do what others think is impossible. Faith fills us to believe and never give up when we are in despair. Faith makes us stronger to overcome those obstacles placed in our path each day. Faith is that immovable force given to us *deep within the soul* to follow and believe in the will of the Lord. In this section, the readings help to give us faith and find strength and courage to know the Lord is always ever present with us as we face our challenges each day.

Thy Brother

NARRATION

Although this prayer is short, it is powerful in what it represents. Picture in your mind Jesus meeting with His apostles for the last time with the setting being on the shore of Lake Galilee. Hear the waves gently crashing; see yourself standing there as Jesus is speaking to His apostles before He ascends into Heaven per the Gospel of John. This prayer is the fulfillment/summation of what Jesus's ministry was about, from His *passion, crucifixion and resurrection*. Jesus was sent to lead us from darkness into the light through His death for the forgiveness of our sins. He lets the apostles know that the Holy Spirit is with them and that the Heavenly Father who sent Him is ever present. As Jesus ascends into Heaven, you hear Him bid the apostles peace, that they go to love and serve the Lord as He did throughout His life and in His ministry with them.

Prayer of Inspiration

Amen! I say to you, brother, my arms are not heavy as I carry you out from the darkness and into the Lord's most holy, glorious light! With the love of the *Holy Spirit* I lift up my hands to our Savior Jesus and hear Him say, "Do not fear, for the God *Our Father* is always near." With outstretched arms and warm embrace, filled with joyous thanks and praise, I say peace be with you, my brother; let us continue our journey to love and serve the Lord.

Amen!

The Journey

NARRATION:
Perhaps nowhere else is the journey to the Lord more diverse than with the apostle Paul. From Paul's example, as he travels to spread the word of the Lord, we can understand that hardship can be overcome. For on our journey, when we lift our burdens up to the Lord, He calms our soul. Jesus's gift of peace and love fills the heart so we are troubled no more as the Spirit guides us along the way to be in His presence.

Prayer of Contemplation

"O my Jesus, how long shall I walk this lonely road of *earthly desires* that consumes me where the cloud of evil overshadows my soul? Lord, help me to release the doubts and fears I hold in the steps I take and let me remove the *great darkness* within my heart. Take me on *Thy journey, Lord*, in searching to be open and in oneness with You. As the journey is long, may I be filled with Your *love placed deep in my heart,* Jesus, and receive the guiding hand of the *Holy Spirit* to follow the *light toward Your glory*." Truly, I say to you, each will undertake his or her own special *journey* to receive a *blessing from the Lord*. Amen! Amen, I say; "With *thanks and praise* that all shall see the wonder in Your ways, most tender Jesus! To this I pray, most *loving, mighty* Lord."

Amen!

The Cross and the Stone

NARRATION:

We see the cross and know the great pain and sacrifice it represents. We praise the resurrection of Jesus, but we miss tying the symbols together as death and life. The *cross can be understood to represent death, while the stone of the tomb can represent the promise of eternal life.* To know this is to recognize one of the mysteries of faith unfolded before us.

Prayer of Reflection

To know of something as unseen and feel that belief within us is a deep hidden truth calling to us. To look upon the cross and see the agony of the faithful Son Jesus, is to behold an image that pierces the heart! It is the symbol of sacrifice to all, a blemished Lamb for the forgiveness of sin and mercy to mankind. The image of the death of one so humble on the cross burns into our spirit and becomes part of our mind, body and soul! They say, "Take this Man's body away; lay Him in the tomb and let the guards stand watch over Him. Roll a stone to seal His tomb where forever He will lay." But on the third day the power of the Kingdom is in His hands, and death cannot overtake His heavenly spirit. Arisen is Jesus, to fulfill Scripture as the temple of the Father. The stone is cast away from the tomb, symbolizing our eternal life through love of the Heavenly Father! Though far apart, they come together; the *cross and the stone, two symbols* in our Christian faith: *one for the end of mortal life and the other for a new beginning of a spiritual life eternal.*

Amen!

Thy Prayers, Even If Delayed, Are Answered, Never Denied

NARRATION

Jesus let us know that we can ask and it shall be given unto us. Sometimes we are caught up in asking for our own wants that we fail to understand that our blessings are given to us or received when we have an open heart. That is when we recognize that, in the asking from our prayer, it will be granted not in our time but in the Lord's time! Having humility and faith in the Lord, we see His goodness in that our wants will always be fulfilled.

Prayer of Inspiration

"Lord, let me appreciate all that has been given unto me. For in my passion, I see the power and the glory You have laid before Thee! Grant me the patience to endure as I await what is and shall be my appointed task. In my heart, Lord, let me know for what I ask is true, that shall be granted to this humble servant from You! Lord, help me to know my prayer(s) are answered, for their outcome may be delayed but never denied as it be fulfilled in Your time. Jesus, I ask for this restless anxiety to be gone as I await the answers to my prayer(s) and receive Your great benefit(s) to be bestowed upon me! Amen! Amen, I say; Jesus, Your faith is my guide to be that constant partner at my side. In this I pray to the Lord most high."

Amen!

Eyes of Faith

NARRATION

After the resurrection, Jesus comes in spirit to the apostles, but they do not recognize Him until He opens their eyes to accept and believe. Although we have not seen, we do believe, for it is faith that gives us courage as we accept the Holy Spirit to guide us on a path to the love of the Lord!

Prayer of Contemplation

"I have come to stand with you, do you not recognize Me? Open thine eyes, cast away your doubt and set your fears aside. Come into My house, that temple of which the Holy Spirit resides to see all that is good and true in *purpose*." Truly, I say to you, what the *Father gives to Man* he must receive; for him to be open, gentle and kind, *filled with love that is Heaven-sent and that can never be bound, as it fills the hearts of many!* Amen! Amen. "I give You thanks and praise, my Lord, and ask, 'O my Jesus, let me have Thine *eyes of faith*, which I seek, to *see in Your heart* and to *feel the love of the merciful Father!*'" In this I pray to the Son of the *Most High* forever eternal.

Amen!

Angels' Slumber

NARRATION:
Picture in the Old Testament the prophets doing the work of the Lord. To speak out in the ways of the Lord was not easy for them. To give them courage and strength, the Lord would lift them up to continue on. So it is with us today also; we must be strong in faith when others will deny us. When we turn ourselves over to the grace of the Lord, He will guide and refresh us with His strength when we need it most.

Prayer of Inspiration

To my Lord I commend my earthly body to rest this day. "I say to You, *God of Heaven*, 'O *my Jesus, O my Jesus, O my Jesus*, hear my cry and protect me from all my fears!' Lord, let Your guiding hand of the *Holy Spirit* come upon me that I may sense its presence to fill my soul. Let all doubt leave me to dispel Satan's thoughts and his attacks against me. With Your strength, I profess, *'Lord, let Your will be done; I am Your humble servant. Satan, depart from me!'* I say to You, Heavenly Father, fill me with Your peace and joy in my heart. May Your *angels' slumber* fall upon this faithful son, giving me rest that I may arise anew to sing Your praises in love and service to You. In this I ask in the name of Your Son Jesus Christ."

Amen!

When Evil Knocks

NARRATION:

From the Gospels, Peter was warned and told by Jesus that he would deny Him. As Peter is in the courtyard after the betrayal of Jesus, he denies Him three times.(13) The temptation of evil won when Peter failed the Lord. Out of fear did Peter turn away and let evil take over. Evil is always wanting us to fail and fall, but Jesus's love for us prevails. With the Holy Spirit and Jesus's great compassion, we are forgiven and restored in faith. When we set our fears aside and trust in the Lord, evil's temptation is overcome.

Prayer of Contemplation

Do I look away and tremble in fear or do I gather courage to face evil? "Let the door be shut, my Lord, for the Spirit to enter through and hold me true. Jesus, cast Your mercy and compassion to forgive my sins for a new start and life with You." Truly, I say to you, evil will knock on the door to open and will tempt the soul. I shall open my arms to receive the Lord and follow His path of peace. Let the Holy Spirit guide and give me strength to never falter. Amen! Amen, I say; evil cannot take what has been given by the Lord but will always want to lead us astray. Stand fast in faith with thanks and praise and be pleasing to the Lord each day.

Amen!

Lift Thy Burdens

NARRATION:
Life is filled with many challenges that one faces each day. How we choose to approach something is within our control. Our emotions can make us view something as hopeless, but we must be disciplined even in the face of an unpleasant task. Jesus knew all too well that our burdens can overwhelm even the strongest of us. With courage, faith and adoration can the Holy Spirit lift one up and make all things possible.

Prayer of Reflection

Frustration fills the heart; one must overcome such emptiness that makes one feel like there is no escape from a meaningless endeavor. Hopelessness dominates the scene, but this is only a temporary setback. Knowing that all is not lost is what drives us forward. Great is the hand that wields the will of the mind to set things right. No shadow of doubt must remain; no fear must hold one back; instead, push on to overcome all that is in front of you! Honor be given to him who is just for a cause, for courage is needed to accomplish that which is required. Let us ache with anticipation to do all that is set before us and achieve what is not thought possible. From within is one's glory known, to grasp the light of the Holy Spirit and be shown the way. Amen, I say; "Bless me, Father, with grace to overcome all burdens I must face."

Amen!

Light of the Lord

NARRATION:
When darkness is revealed by the light shined upon it, man is set free. Evil hides its true purpose within a lie to hold men captive. With Jesus, the cause of justice for the salvation of the soul is put forth in *Divine principle* that cannot be denied. In the Holy Spirit all is revealed, so that man is free to reject Satan's deeds.

Prayer of Contemplation

The light of the Lord shines forth for a *new dawn* to appear. Hearts are touched and souls set free that are awakened to see the *devil's crushed tyranny. Alleluia!* Rejoice and be glad; shed a tear for this be the day the *hand of Providence* is here… for righteous people come forth to make a stand for this land, anointed with the *Spirit of the Lord*. Truly, I say, the fight is not over, but a great battle is won as our *faith* be restored to put Satan's evil on the run. Amen! Amen, I say, when good men come together in common thought and bond for a *Divine purpose*, evil shall perish and be vanquished unto the end. In this I pray in the name of Jesus, to let all see the light of the Lord!

Amen!

Cobwebs

NARRATION:
When we are most in despair and feel hopeless and abandoned by the Lord is when we should turn back. Such is the case for Job; in losing everything, he feels lost and forsaken. Only when one can clear a path (remove the cobwebs) to be open from the *heart* will a *new spark of faith and energy be driven by the Holy Spirit*. As Job was lost, so are we at times, but the power of the Holy Spirit brings new life and faith to us all. With the Spirit's touch we can see and feel the goodness of the Lord and forever blessed be!

Prayer of Reflection

When we let the *dust and cobwebs* of inaction gather in our *heart and mind*, are we not cut off? Blow the dust away and sweep the cobwebs clean to rekindle the fire that was once so brightly lit. *Come, Thou Holy Spirit*, and strike me now from where I sit! For I have fallen away, but now the cloud of dust has been removed from my chest. My *mind and heart* are open now to see the *glory, love and compassion of Jesus* that I might stay. Truly, I say to you, when *hearts, minds and eyes are opened*, no wonder is too small or feat so great than that of the Lord whom we celebrate. Amen! Amen, let the *bounty of the Spirit* come to all and remove the cobwebs from *our soul* that each may see the *light of the Lord to burn forever bright!*

Amen!

Love is the joy within that is forever eternal.

Part IV
Receiving Love

**Pray with *openness*;
let His love fill the *heart*!**

Love is known as the greatest emotion of all, for it is said that "love conquers all." Love is the internal happiness and joy that we feel in the heart.

Webster's dictionary defines *love* as "unselfish loyal and benevolent… concern for the good of another: such as the fatherly concern of God for humankind."(14)

In my personal view, *love* is "a Spiritual Bliss and strong emotion within each of us that has no bounds for Love is not tied to the *Earthly Realm* as it can transcend from *Life to Death* and outward to the *Heavens*." In this section the prayers help us to feel and embrace the *love* that Jesus has for us as we accept His *joy and happiness from His love into our heart*.

Step to Heaven

NARRATION:
This poem is dedicated to all those whom we have lost in this life as we remember them with love and kindness so that they will not be forgotten, for theirs is a place of rest and eternal happiness.

Inspiration

Is not the question I ask *when I should go*, for it is the journey that I make? Slowly moving throughout this *plane of earthly life*, if only for a short while. Stopping and smiling at the passersby, bringing joy and happiness to all around, only to come to the *end of this life's great road* wanting to take another turn! Fleeting is the time given to make my presence known, but to Him who sent me I am shown. For now I must leave this *earthly shore*, for I am called to *step to Heaven* for eternal life evermore.

Love of Joy

NARRATION

Picture Jesus in your mind and hear Him speaking to the apostles, saying to them, "Be open to Him who sent Me." As Jesus was teaching the Beatitudes, you can feel a softer message of joy that lies within them. This prayer was written to let each of us know how to receive the *love of joy* and to know that joy can be found anywhere if we but look. When we *open our heart and see the goodness all around* us, that is joy of the spirit within us. To be *thankful for those in our life to have* to share with, that is joy. To say *thank you to someone for an act of kindness* is joy. Joy is a subtle thing but is all around us.

Prayer of Contemplation

"Jesus, what do we say to each other? Let us stop to ask how we can bring joy to one another. Lord, help us to understand our great purpose to know what joy is and how it can be found within us." I say, *amen,* and let *Heaven's* praises come softly unto me! In the quiet of His presence, the *Eternal Father* does respond; the *love of joy* lies within our *heart* when we are but filled with *love, kindness, compassion, forgiveness and mercy* as *Christ our Heavenly King.* Truly, I say to you, "Lord, may we always know the joy within a humble *heart!*"

Amen!

Gift of Passion and Purpose

NARRATION

We often find a struggle within ourselves, wondering what we are meant to be, for we all have a calling to fulfill a need within life. This *passion and purpose* lies within each of us; if we look to accept it, then it will be shown to us through the gift of *love and the grace of our Lord*.

Prayer of Reflection

To follow a path that others doubt is to believe in oneself. It is a certainty to give *purpose* from deep within; Divine meaning that opens the soul to receive a call. With *burning passion* we come alive to find our way, that path given to us that no one can take away. Amen, I say to you, "Lord, with *humility, gratitude, and praise*, let me accept my *gift, my one true passion and purpose* I am meant to follow; to receive joy and happiness in this life to not be hollow, but filled with peace and void of strife. For this I pray to You, my loving Lord Jesus Christ."

Amen!

Love Thyself

NARRATION:
As Jesus teaches in the New Testament, one needs *love* to be open to Him. Love is a powerful force that gives us courage to be faithful, obedient, compassionate and caring within ourselves, toward others and unto the Lord.

Prayer of Inspiration

Truly, I say to you, *joy of the heart* can come when one "*loves thyself.*" To be faithful and obedient to the Lord, one must have *love in the heart*. The *spirit of love* must be nurtured like a flower that blooms, showing its beauty to all. Jesus always taught *love* to those around Him, expressing that forgiveness comes from the *love* within. When people know love, accept love and can express love for themselves and others, great blessings occur. Those who miss this *golden point of Jesus* fail to find the fulfillment they seek. Amen! Amen, I say, that *love be accepted into one's heart* to make it full of kindness and compassion. In this I pray to the most beloved Son Jesus Christ.

Amen!

Refresh My Soul

NARRATION

To overcome despair, one must be thankful and know that help is always there. For our *faith will guide us,* to *give hope* that any troubles we face can be pushed aside. For *Jesus's love* is there always at our side, to lift us up *through His Spirit* if we just call out His name to *refresh the soul.*

Prayer of Contemplation

"The *depths of despair* are a heavy weight that pulls me down, my Lord. Give comfort and courage to me so that I will *lift this burden from me!* By Your *compassionate hand shall my faith be strong* like a *bar of iron and hope fill my soul* to overcome all before me. *Pour out Your Spirit to refresh my soul, loving Lord,* as I go forth." Truly, I say, the *Lord's power and might is great* that all shall receive *His love and be guided toward His eternal light.* "To Thee do we come, Jesus, to be a child who is favored in Thy Father's sight. Amen! Amen, I say, that *thanks and praise* be given unto You, O Lord, as You *protect and guide us* that we may always do what is right! In this I pray, most gracious and loving *Lord Jesus Christ.*"

Amen!

Devil's Shadow

NARRATION:
The shadow of evil takes many forms that we do not always see. We fall prey to the devil's desires to take us away from the Lord. With the helping hand of Jesus's love *and the Holy Spirit, His compassion will guide us back and deliver us from harm.*

Prayer of Contemplation

"Cast out the *devil's shadow from my soul, O Lord!* Enter Your *love upon my heart that I may once again have joy.* Let me push away the *sinful deeds of man that consume him.* For You are just, my Lord, *and give the Holy Spirit to let one see!*" Truly, I say to you, *lies and destruction hold the evil man captive in the dark to never be free.* "Lord, may Your grace and love guide the hand to lead with justice. Jesus, *let Your compassion and mercy fill the heart, mind and soul so all receive Your love.* Amen! Amen, I say; *O Lord, Your glory is forever.* Let us be *wise in spirit* to go forth and *love one another.*" In this I pray to Jesus Christ the Lord, *that all will be free from Satan's strife and walk toward a holy life.*

Amen!

Thy Spirit of Peace and Love

NARRATION:
When we read the Lord's words, we search deep for their meaning. Only when we are open to hear and listen do we understand, for a *beacon of light turns on*, leading us to receive the *gifts of peace and love* that touch deep within the heart.

Prayer of Inspiration

"Let me listen to Your *sacred Word*, my Lord, that I shall hear. May my *heart, mind, body, soul and Divinity* be cast as one, Jesus, to understand the meaning of Your *power and glory*! From the *eyes of Thine prophets* shall I see and know, as it will be from the *faith planted deep within me*. Truly, I say, my Lord, Your words give comfort and courage for each to be open that he or she will know Your *spirit of peace and love*. Amen! Amen, I say, with thanks and praise my Lord's will shall be done to *touch the heart* of all, that all be *united as one*! In this I pray to my *loving Lord Jesus Christ*.

Amen!

Heart of Fire

NARRATION:
Jesus speaks of *love to fill and burn within the heart*. It is through *love* that we understand and know compassion for each other. Having *love in the heart* for others will help give us the *peace we seek*.

Prayer of Reflection

How can a *man be a man* if he is not open to the Lord? If a *heart* is cold is it like the *winter frost*? Let your *heart be on fire* like the ambers of the *blacksmith's forge* to burn with *desire for the love of the Father*! Truly, I say to you, a heart filled *with love* is most favored by the Lord. "Jesus, let no boundary keep one back to seek and find Your *love*." Amen! Amen, I say, to the *Word of my Lord*, for Jesus does say His peace be with us; go to *love and serve the Lord*. "For this I pray, Lord, that *peace and love* fill the *heart* of all who ask and accept Your task."

Amen!

Thy Need Fulfilled

NARRATION

When we are frustrated or feel lonely and angry, the Lord is there to help us if we ask, as in the example of Job. When we open our heart to Jesus, He knows our faults and is there to forgive. Through His great *love and compassion,* He touches us so that we may weep with *joy in our heart.* As we accept Jesus and know that He is with us always, no situation can be so bleak or dark that it cannot be overcome. The *love from the Lord conquers all,* so when we put our faith in Him, He is with us always.

Prayer of Contemplation

"In my *darkest hour* do I turn to the *Lord on high;* I have tread so long on this lonely path. When others turn away for their own selfish pleasures, I sense a presence to come from You, *O my Jesus.* In the depths of my despair, I know not fear, for my faith has brought me near to *open my heart unto You!* Trials and tribulations will be nothing compared to the *love You have for all.* With praise do I ask, and with gratitude in my heart; no worries will be found, for all shall be overcome—with You, Lord, my need is fulfilled." Amen! Amen, I say unto you, "*O Lord,* let Your *glory, love and peace fill me always.*" No troubles shall ever keep me away from my Lord, as His compassion has shown me the way!

Amen!

Voice from the Heart

NARRATION

Call it intuition or that feeling we have that guides us, this is the voice from the *heart* that calls out to each of us. This is the internal voice of reason and is a guardian for us. The voice is that of a protector and counselor, if we are open to listen and understand. It is a spirit of wisdom given to each of us *with great love and by* the *blessing of the Lord.*

Inspiration

Let us be open to gather in spirit, to feel the *heartbeat* in the pulse of love. Calmly and silently does each pulse speak, giving the *breath of life*. The wonder of our Lord is ever present within the *heart*. Listen and you shall hear that *"voice of the heart"* calling you near. Truly, I say, people never falter when they stay true, embracing *faith and love* as they shall be guided by this voice forever new each day. May Jesus shine His light on all who understand this *mystery of the heart,* that *voice in spirit* pulling us close to never be apart.

Sing praises to the Lord with shouts of joy!

Part V
Embracing the Spirit

**Pray often in thanksgiving to the Heavenly Father;
let the Spirit come to you!**

The Spirit is a soft-calling voice, a guide to lead us on our journey when we are ready to listen. Let the Spirit come to you and receive the gifts it will bestow. From the *Spirit*, each one is given a unique passion and purpose in the eyes of the Lord. May these readings help reflect on the *glory, the power, the Spirit and the Kingdom of the Father.*

Redemption

NARRATION: (Mark 9:23-29)

In prayer all things are possible if we trust in Him. Faith is given in belief that from prayer our demons are released. Picture Jesus's apostles trying to cast out demons from the people. See them standing there laying hands on and speaking over those gathered before them. The apostles are not able to release this one demon. Jesus walks up and speaks to the boy's father, asking him if he has faith. The father says he does and asks a prayer for mercy. Jesus steps forward and casts the demon out of the son. Jesus says to the apostles that this demon can only be cast out through prayer.

Prayer of Contemplation

Do our eyes not see or our ears not hear the *glory of the Lord*? Truly I say to you, your faith will restore you. Thy work is never-ending; *praise be to Him who will save my soul*! "Jesus, cast out my *demons* that through my prayers Your good works abide. *I pray, Lord, to let me go forth and be healed by Your tender touch as You redeem my heart, forgive my sins and share Your everlasting love for me.* Amen, I say; *Jesus, let me not hide as I am called to stand by Your side.* O Heavenly Father, for my belief let me see all things are possible as I give my faith and prayers unto You."

Amen!

Essence Divine

NARRATION:
In the Bible, buried in the words of Jabez, the apostle Peter, King David's psalms and other prophets are supernatural secrets to life eternal.(15) In these words, we can see, feel and know that *essence is given by faith and the power of the Holy Spirit.*

Prayer of Inspiration

"Blessed is the one who comes in the *name* of the *Lord (Hosanna!)*; we ask You to send *prosperity*. O my Jesus, bless me that Your hand keep me from *harm. I pray to You that I find favor in Your sight, my Lord, and come to know Your ways.* For I confess to You, Jesus, my faults…that I need Your *love in my heart* so I shall believe! To the *glory of the Father* I kneel and ask: descend Your Spirit of wisdom, knowledge and revelation upon me to be enlightened in *passion and purpose of Your richness in heart and soul.*" Truly, I say, shall the *Holy Spirit* project its power to strengthen the *inner man to be rooted and grounded in love.* Amen! Amen, I say; shall the *passion of the Holy Spirit* impart to me what is the *breadth, length, height and depth* of the fullness of *love in Christ and the essence of the eternal Heavenly Father upon me!*

Amen!

Green Pasture

NARRATION: (Psalm 23)

"The Lord is my shepherd"; we seek to find Him. With openness and love in our heart, Jesus will guide us and come to us. Peace and calm will surround the *soul* as we are refreshed in spirit from the *pasture of the Lord*!

Prayer of Contemplation

Out of the *desert* I have come, to seek the *green pasture* of the Lord, with *eyes to see, ears to hear and lips to speak the glory of my Lord Jesus Christ*. "Fill me with the strength of Moses from *his staff of faith* and let Your miracles be done through me, O Lord! *Blessed be this day*, for the *light has touched my soul* to know the comfort of Your arms. Let Your bounty come forth to me, *O my Jesus,* to grow and prosper, for thanks and praise I give to You all my days." Amen! Amen, I say; lead me into His green pasture where I will go, for this be my Lord's promise to make it so.

Amen!

Together We Pray

NARRATION:
Jesus would often pray to the Father in solitude and seek His guidance. In prayer we can hear our thoughts and get direction for our needs. The *spiritual power and beauty of prayer is often overlooked*, but as one embraces it, prayer changes the *heart, mind and soul*, giving us a new outlook and understanding.

Prayer of Inspiration

"Blessed are those who gather to *pray together in Your name, Jesus*. They will become one with the *Trinity of the Father, Son and Holy Spirit in Thy Kingdom to come!* In *prayer united to a common cause* do we the faithful stand, as Thy will be done. Let the Holy Spirit call out to *place love, compassion and forgiveness within our heart*." Amen! Amen, I say; let the *power of prayer* be known so that all will understand its beauty and, through the *Holy Spirit*, be shown the *light of its grace*. In this we pray, most loving Savior Lord Jesus Christ.

Amen!

Rise Up in Spirit

NARRATION:
We often say, "*Come, Holy Spirit,*" but are we truly open to receive it? The Spirit does come when we least expect it to shine its light upon us. For as it does, we shall *rise up in spirit* and be not afraid to shout it out. This is the gift given to us; the *Lord has spoken to fill our heart, mind and soul so it shall never be broken.*

Prayer of Reflection

On the road, I was all alone till a stranger did pass me by. For what I did not know, but this stranger caught my *eye*. I could sense and feel a familiar face, a person full of *love and amazing grace*! As I approached, I heard Him say, "*Rise up; the Spirit comes your way.*" A strong glow came forth, and again I heard Him say, "*Look away, look away,* for it is the *Spirit* that comes upon you *today*!" Touched with a *joyous light* that pierces deep into the *soul*, I am told "*Rise up in the Holy Spirit's embrace,* go forth and shout it out to all this day!"

Amen!

Embrace each new day,
that it may always
fill the heart with kindness
and compassion.

Special Inspirations

**Pray and embrace the words of the Father,
for you shall have joy and happiness in the heart!**

In deep thought we seek to understand the meanings behind the written words of the Bible. From the words of King David in the Psalms, can we as men find inspiration? His words speak to the heart as we work to discover and embrace their meaning.

Also within the Bible are examples of women who faced struggles for themselves and others. Perhaps the greatest is the Virgin Mary. She accepted the Lord's request to be the handmaiden of the Lord. Through her *faith* and trust in the Lord, she received the Immaculate Conception and gave birth to our Lord Jesus. Like men, women also need inspiration to gather courage and be strengthened in faith.

As men and women, we come together in love to share a bond that is the foundation for the family. From this unity children shall spring forth, each a *blessing* from the Lord.

Each reading that follows shows that men and women can call on the Holy Spirit to give them strength and guidance toward God's love and to fulfill their roles as part of the sacred family in God's Kingdom.

That Man Is You! (TMIY)

NARRATION:

King David from his psalms works to be a *man after God's own heart*. He knows his faults and works to correct them. We as men are challenged to find our place and direction in life. When we seek to fulfill God's desire and accept our role in the family and society, we become the kind of man—TMIY!—that the Lord intended. The Lord's grace comes upon us when we strive to follow His basic tenants as part of our daily lives in all that we do.

Prayer for Inspiration
(Written by a TMIY Participant)

"Lord, I ask that You give me Your strength to comfort those in need and guide me as You did Your apostles. Give me *courage* to confront the challenges I shall face and be a witness in faith. Lord, fill me with Your *Holy Spirit* that I will live up to the life You have given me and grant me the *passion of King David* to be a man after Your own *heart*! Help me fulfill God's original desire to be *'That Man Is You' with clarity of thought, integrity of action, honesty of heart and purity of love*. I ask this through Jesus Christ our Savior; for this I pray!"

Amen!

The Woman in Faith (TWIF)

NARRATION:

From the New Testament, we can see that Mary is a role model for women as they face struggles in their daily lives. Mary approached life with a humble heart as the handmaiden of the Lord as she was filled with the Holy Spirit and stayed true in her love and devotion to Jesus and the Heavenly Father.

Prayer for Inspiration

"I ask You, Jesus, to make me enlightened to Your mysteries of faith and love for the Father. Send forth the *power of the Holy Spirit* upon me that it may guide me with eternal wisdom! Let me not be afraid to confront the *challenges* You place before me, Lord, and bear witness to my faith. Lord, may I be '*That Woman in Faith*' to fulfill God's desire—filled with devotion, love and compassion to be a woman after Your own heart, Lord! May You guide me, Heavenly Father, with *clarity of thought, integrity of action, honesty of heart and purity of love* in all that I do! I ask this in the name of Your Son Jesus Christ."

Amen!

You are the fountain and
Jesus is the water; come
and taste the Spirit of life.

Conclusion

Know all things are possible with the *power of prayer*, as you will be *blessed in spirit with compassion and love from Jesus the Son and the Heavenly Father*!

Do we know prayer as the Lord calls us to? The power of prayer is in the simplicity that comes from the heart. As the Spirit shows us the will of the Lord, wise counsel and wisdom shall be found in prayer to listen, hear and understand the words of the Lord.

We each have a battle within us as we struggle to find inner peace. In this battle, we can use prayer as a tool to help us grow spiritually to find that harmony within us. To those who say prayer is not important, I would like to say it is for each person to decide. Prayer is the *spiritual guidance* to direct the *soul* toward a *higher self*.

Remember, the Lord is with you always; you just need to call out His name. Speak to the Lord often using prayer as He calls us to know Him. The Lord will reveal His wonders and mysteries if we but speak to Him and listen with an open *heart*. May you always be at peace to love the Lord and let prayer be your guide to ask for forgiveness and discover the essence of the Lord.

The emotional steps we take on our journey are like the colors within nature; they constantly change to show us the breadth of life. On this quest for *spiritual growth and maturity,* using prayer, we can discover great *wisdom, grace, faith and love,* to fill the *heart and soul* with *passion and joy*. After reading this book and taking my journey with me, may it inspire you to reach out and embrace prayer. Let your "*Voice from the Heart*" be your guide as you take a "*Walk with the Spirit,*" *embracing the love of Christ* to find comfort and using prayer to overcome your *spiritual battle*.

REFERENCES

(1) *Merriam-Webster Online*, s.v. "wisdom," accessed July 19, 2021, https://www.merriam-webster.com/dictionary/wisdom. The definition of *wisdom* is as follows:

1 a: ability to discern inner qualities and relationships: INSIGHT
b: good sense: JUDGMENT
c: generally accepted belief
// challenges what has become accepted *wisdom* among many historians — Robert Darnton
d: accumulated philosophical or scientific learning: KNOWLEDGE
2: a wise attitude, belief, or course of action
3: the teachings of the ancient wise men

(2) Here are some verses from Proverbs regarding *strife*:

Proverbs 15:18
A wrathful man stirreth up strife: but he that is slow to anger appeaseth strife.

Proverbs 16:28
A froward man soweth strife: and a whisperer separateth chief friends.

Proverbs 17:1
Better is a dry morsel, and quietness therewith, than a house full of sacrifices with strife.

Proverbs 20:3
It is an honor for a man to cease from strife: but every fool will be meddling.

(3) Here are some verses from Proverbs regarding *anger*:

Proverbs 15:1
A soft answer turneth away wrath: but grievous words stir up anger.

Proverbs 15:18
A wrathful man stirreth up strife: but he that is slow to anger appeaseth strife.

Proverbs 16:32
He that is slow to anger is better than the mighty; and he that ruleth his spirit than he that taketh a city.

Proverbs 19:11
The discretion of a man deferreth his anger; and it is his glory to pass over a transgression.

Proverbs 27:4
Wrath is cruel, and anger is outrageous; but who is able to stand before envy?

(4) Here are some scriptures about the gift of the Holy Spirit:

Mark 16:15
And he said unto them, Go ye into all the world, and preach the gospel to every creature.

Luke 24:49
And, behold, I send the promise of my Father upon you: but tarry ye in the city of Jerusalem, until ye be endued with power from on high.

Matthew 28:20
Teaching them to observe all things whatsoever I have commanded you: and, lo, I am with you always, even unto the end of the world. Amen.

(5) Here are some scriptures about Job:

Job 42:8
Therefore, take unto you now seven bullocks and seven rams, and go to my servant Job, and offer up for yourselves a burnt offering; and my servant Job shall pray for you: for him will I accept: lest I deal with you after your folly, in that ye have not spoken of me the thing which is right, like my servant Job.

Job 42:10
And the Lord turned the captivity of Job, when he prayed for his friends: also, the Lord gave Job twice as much as he had before.

Job 42:12
So, the Lord blessed the latter end of Job more than his beginning: for he had fourteen thousand sheep, and six thousand camels, and a thousand yoke of oxen, and a thousand she asses.

(6) Following are some examples from the Book of Daniel:

Daniel 6:27
He delivereth and rescueth, and he worketh signs and wonders in heaven and in earth, who hath delivered Daniel from the power of the lions.

Daniel 10:11-12
And he said unto me, O Daniel, a man greatly beloved, understand the words that I speak unto thee, and stand upright: for unto thee am I now sent. And when he had spoken this word unto me, I stood trembling. Then said he unto me, Fear not, Daniel: for from the first day that thou didst set thine heart to understand, and to chasten thyself before thy God, thy words were heard, and I am come for thy words.

(7) *Merriam-Webster Online*, s.v., "grace," accessed July 20, 2021, https://www.merriam-webster.com/dictionary/grace. The definition of *grace* is as follows:

1 a: unmerited divine assistance given to humans for their regeneration or sanctification
b: a virtue coming from God
c: a state of sanctification enjoyed through divine assistance

(8) Here is what Jesus said about children:

Matthew 18:5
And whoso shall receive one such little child in my name receiveth me.

(9) Here are some scriptures about Jesus's healing of the blind:

Luke 4:18
The Spirit of the LORD is upon me, because he hath anointed me to preach the gospel to the poor; he hath sent me to heal the brokenhearted, to preach deliverance to the captives, and recovering of sight to the blind, to set at liberty them that are bruised.

John 9:1
And as Jesus passed by, he saw a man which was blind from his birth.

John 9:6-7
When he had thus spoken, he spat on the ground, and made clay of the spittle, and he anointed the eyes of the blind man with the clay, And said unto him, Go, wash in the pool of Siloam, (which is by interpretation, Sent.) He went his way therefore, and washed, and came seeing.

Matthew 12:22
Then was brought unto him one possessed with a devil, blind, and dumb: and he healed him, insomuch that the blind and dumb both spake and saw.

(10) Following are some scriptures regarding solitary, quiet prayer:

Luke 9:18
And it came to pass, as he was alone praying, his disciples were with him: and he asked them, saying, Whom say the people that I am?

Luke 9:36
And when the voice was past, Jesus was found alone. And they kept it close, and told no man in those days any of those things which they had seen.

Luke 11:1
And it came to pass, that, as he was praying in a certain place, when he ceased, one of his disciples said unto him, Lord, teach us to pray, as John also taught his disciples.

(11) *Merriam-Webster Online*, s.v., "faith," accessed July 24, 2021, www.merriam-webster.com/dictionary/faith. The definition of *faith* is as follows:

1 a: allegiance to duty or a person: LOYALTY
// lost *faith* in the company's president
b (1): fidelity to one's promises
(2): sincerity of intentions
// acted in good *faith*
2 a (1): belief and trust in and loyalty to God
(2): belief in the traditional doctrines of a religion
b (1): firm belief in something for which there is no proof
// clinging to the *faith* that her missing son would one day return
(2): complete trust
3: something that is believed especially with strong conviction
especially: a system of religious beliefs
// the Protestant *faith*

(12) Here is the scripture about this woman's faith:

Matthew 15:28
Then Jesus answered and said unto her, O woman, great is thy faith: be it unto thee even as thou wilt. And her daughter was made whole from that very hour.

(13) Here are some scriptures regarding Peter's temptation:

Matthew 26:34
Jesus said unto him, Verily I say unto thee, That this night, before the cock crow, thou shalt deny me thrice.

Matthew 26:75
And Peter remembered the word of Jesus, which said unto him, Before the cock crow, thou shalt deny me thrice. And he went out, and wept bitterly.

(14) *Merriam-Webster Online*, s.v., "love," accessed July 26, 2021, https://www.merriam-webster.com/dictionary/love. The definition of *love* is as follows:

1 a (1): strong affection for another arising out of kinship or personal ties…
(3): affection based on admiration, benevolence, or common interests…

3 a: the object of attachment, devotion, or admiration...
4 a: unselfish loyal and benevolent (see BENEVOLENT sense 1a) concern for the good of another: such as
(1): the fatherly concern of God for humankind
(2): brotherly concern for others
b: a person's adoration of God

(15) Here are some of those words about supernatural secrets to life eternal:

1 Chronicles 4:10
And Jabez called on the God of Israel, saying, Oh that thou wouldest bless me indeed, and enlarge my coast, and that thine hand might be with me, and that thou wouldest keep me from evil, that it may not grieve me! And God granted him that which he requested.

2 Peter 1:3
According as his divine power hath given unto us all things that pertain unto life and godliness, through the knowledge of him that hath called us to glory and virtue.

Psalm 9:1
I will praise thee, O LORD, with my whole heart; I will shew forth all thy marvellous works.

Psalm 21:7
For the king trusteth in the LORD, and through the mercy of the most High he shall not be moved.

NOTES